Endangered Frogs

Molly Aloian & Bobbie Kalman

Crabtree Publishing Company

www.crabtreebooks.com

Earth's Endangered Animals Series
A Bobbie Kalman Book

Dedicated by Molly Aloian
For James De Swert, who has hopped his way into my heart.

Editor-in-Chief
Bobbie Kalman

Writing team
Molly Aloian
Bobbie Kalman

Substantive editor
Kathryn Smithyman

Editors
Robin Johnson
Kelley MacAulay
Rebecca Sjonger

Design
Katherine Kantor
Samantha Crabtree (front cover)

Production coordinator
Heather Fitzpatrick

Photo research
Crystal Foxton

Consultant
Patricia Loesche, Ph.D., Animal Behavior Program,
Department of Psychology, University of Washington

Illustrations
Bonna Rouse: back cover, pages 7, 9

Photographs
Animals Animals - Earth Scenes: © ABPL/Patterson, Rod: page 13 (top);
    © Bernard, George: page 8; © Dennis, David M.: page 29;
    © Ingram, Stephen: page 26; © Kent, Breck P.: page 20;
    © Sheldon, Allen Blake: page 28
Bruce Coleman Inc.: Kim Taylor: page 17
iStockphoto.com: Marcus Brown: page 27; Norman Chan: page 12;
    Steffen Foerster: page 22; Richard Gunion: page 30; Ula Kapala:
    page 14 (bottom)
© Dwight Kuhn: page 16
Photo Researchers, Inc.: E. R. Degginger: page 25; C. K. Lorenz: page 23;
    Stuart Wilson: page 19
Michael P. Turco: pages 4, 18
© Joe McDonald/Visuals Unlimited: page 24
Other images by Digital Vision and TongRo Image Stock

Crabtree Publishing Company

www.crabtreebooks.com   1-800-387-7650

Cataloging-in-Publication Data
Aloian, Molly.
    Endangered frogs / Molly Aloian & Bobbie Kalman.
       p. cm. -- (Earth's endangered animals)
    Includes index.
    ISBN-13: 978-0-7787-1872-7 (rlb)
    ISBN-10: 0-7787-1872-7 (rlb)
    ISBN-13: 978-0-7787-1918-2 (pbk)
    ISBN-10: 0-7787-1918-9 (pbk)
    1. Frogs--Juvenile literature. 2. Endangered species--Juvenile literature.
I. Kalman, Bobbie. II. Title.
    QL668.E2A46 2006
    597.8'9--dc22
                                                                    2005036720
                                                                    LC

**Published in
the United States**

PMB16A
350 Fifth Ave.
Suite 3308
New York, NY
10118

**Published
in Canada**

616 Welland Ave.
St. Catharines, Ontario
Canada
L2M 5V6

**Published in the
United Kingdom**

White Cross Mills
High Town, Lancaster
LA1 4XS
United Kingdom

**Published
in Australia**

386 Mt. Alexander Rd.
Ascot Vale (Melbourne)
VIC 3032

Contents

Endangered frogs

Frogs are **endangered** animals. Today, there are only about 4,000 **species**, or types, of frogs on Earth. In the past, however, many thousands of species of frogs lived on Earth. It is difficult for scientists to know when a frog species becomes endangered. Scientists know that certain changes in the environment are dangerous to frogs, but they are not sure how many frog species are at risk of becoming **extinct**. Keep reading to find out the reasons why so many frogs are endangered and how people can help these animals.

Scientists believe that frogs have been living on Earth for at least 190 million years.

Words to know

Scientists use specific words to describe animals that are in danger. Some of these words are listed here.

vulnerable Describes animals that may become endangered because they face dangers in the **wild**, or natural areas not controlled by people

endangered Describes animals that are in danger of dying out in the wild

critically endangered Describes animals that are at high risk of dying out in the wild

extinct Describes animals that have died out or animals that have not been seen in the wild for at least 50 years

If people do not work to protect frogs, many more species, such as this red-legged frog, will become extinct.

What are frogs?

Frogs are **amphibians**. Amphibians are **cold-blooded** animals. The body temperatures of cold-blooded animals change as the temperatures of their surroundings change. For example, when a frog sits in the sun, its body temperature becomes warm. When a frog sits in the shade, its body temperature becomes cool.

No tails

Frogs belong to an **order**, or group, of amphibians called *Anura*. Toads are animals that also belong to the Anura group. The word "Anura" means "no tail." Frogs and toads are amphibians that do not have tails. Other amphibians, such as newts and salamanders, have tails.

Bones in their backs

All amphibians are **vertebrates**. Vertebrates are animals that have **backbones**. A backbone is a row of bones down the middle of an animal's back.

Two lives

The word "amphibian" means "two lives." An amphibian lives one part of its life in water and the other part of its life on land. When it is young, a frog lives and finds food mainly in water. When it is fully grown, a frog lives and finds food mainly on land.

frog

toad

Frog or toad?

Frogs and toads are both called anurans because they belong to the Anura group. There are only a few differences between frogs and toads. What differences can you see in the pictures above? Most toads have shorter back legs than frogs do. Toads usually have bumpy, dry skin, whereas frogs usually have smooth, wet skin. Frogs are excellent jumpers, whereas toads often walk.

A frog's life cycle

Every animal goes through a set of changes from the time it is born or hatches from an egg to the time it is an adult. This set of changes is called a **life cycle**. A frog's life cycle begins inside an egg. A **tadpole**, or young frog, hatches from the egg. The young frog goes through many changes as it grows into an adult.

In fact, a frog's body changes completely during the frog's life cycle. The set of changes that a frog's body goes through is called **metamorphosis**. When a frog has finished its metamorphosis, it is a **mature**, or an adult, frog. An adult frog can **mate**, or join together, with another frog to make babies.

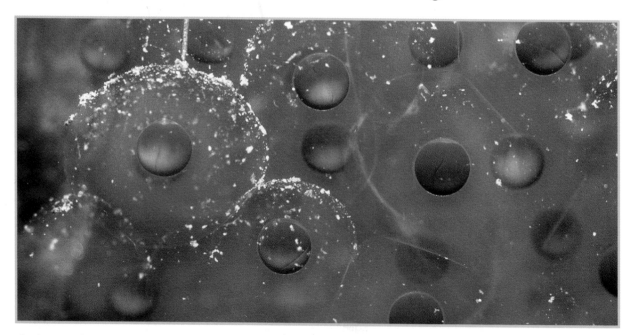

*A tiny **embryo**, or developing animal, is growing inside each of these frog eggs.*

The life cycle of a frog

A female frog usually lays eggs in water. She can lay thousands of eggs at once! After about a week, a tadpole hatches from each egg. The tadpole lives in water and has **gills** for breathing under water, just as a fish does. The tadpole has a long tail. After about ten weeks, the tadpole grows legs, and its tail begins to shrink.

Skin begins to grow over the tadpole's gills. **Lungs** grow inside its body. The tadpole now lives on land and breathes air using its lungs. It has short front and **hind**, or back, legs. As the tadpole continues to grow, its tail becomes shorter. A frog is finished metamorphosis when it no longer has a tail. It is now an adult frog.

A frog is mature when it is between twelve and sixteen weeks old.

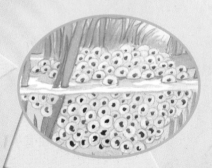

Frog eggs are called **spawn**. *They are covered in clear, soft jelly.*

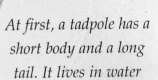

At first, a tadpole has a short body and a long tail. It lives in water and eats plants.

The tadpole soon lives on land and breathes air using its lungs. Its tail is nearly gone.

The tadpole grows legs, and its tail begins to shrink.

9

Where do frogs live?

Frogs live in many parts of the world. They live on every **continent** except Antarctica. Most frogs, such as the tree frog shown above, live in **tropical regions**. Tropical regions are areas of the Earth that are near the **equator**. The equator is an imaginary line around the center of the Earth. In tropical regions, the weather is hot and **humid**, or moist, year round.

10

Hot and cold

Some frogs live in **temperate regions**, or areas of the Earth where the seasons change during the year. Temperate regions have hot summers and cold winters.

No action

Many frogs that live in temperate regions survive hot summers or cold winters by living in **burrows**, or underground homes. While they are in their burrows, frogs go into an inactive state called **torpor**. They stop eating and move very little. Their heartbeats slow down to help their bodies **conserve**, or save, energy. When the weather is suitable, the frogs come out of their burrows to look for food.

This red-legged frog lives in a temperate region.

Frog habitats

Different species of frogs live in different **habitats**. A habitat is the natural place where an animal lives. Many frogs live in forests—especially **rain forests**. A rain forest is a hot, thick forest in a tropical region. Rain forests receive at least 80 inches (203 cm) of rain each year. Some frogs live in **grasslands** and in deserts. Most frogs live close to water, however. They live near creeks, ponds, streams, and **wetlands**. A wetland is an area of land that is **waterlogged**, or soaked with water, for part or all of the year. Marshes and swamps are two types of wetlands in which frogs live.

*Many frogs live in or near bodies of water such as lakes, rivers, ponds, and **bogs**. A bog is wet, muddy ground.*

Heat factor

Some frogs live in deserts. In order to escape the hot, dry weather, these frogs live in underground burrows and go into torpor. They may remain in torpor for up to ten months of the year! When it rains and the weather cools, the frogs become active again.

This African bullfrog lives in the Kalahari Desert in the southern part of Africa.

Trees, please

Other frogs, called tree frogs, live in the trees of rain forests and other forests. Tree frogs are excellent climbers and are often very small. A few species of tree frogs do not spend their entire lives in trees. These tree frogs live in tall grasses on the ground.

The red-eyed tree frog lives in the rain forests of Central America.

The pads on this tree frog's toes stick to the surfaces on which the frog climbs.

This aquatic frog is using its webbed feet to push itself through water.

Frog bodies

Frogs have bodies that are suited to their habitats. Different species have different body parts that help them survive in their habitats.

Different bodies

Tree frogs have sticky pads on their toes. They use the pads to hold on to branches and leaves while they climb trees. Frogs that live in deserts often have strong legs for digging burrows. Some frogs that live in deserts can store water in their bodies. These frogs use the stored water during **droughts**, or long periods without rain. **Aquatic frogs**, or frogs that live only in water, are great swimmers. They use their **webbed** feet to swim quickly through water.

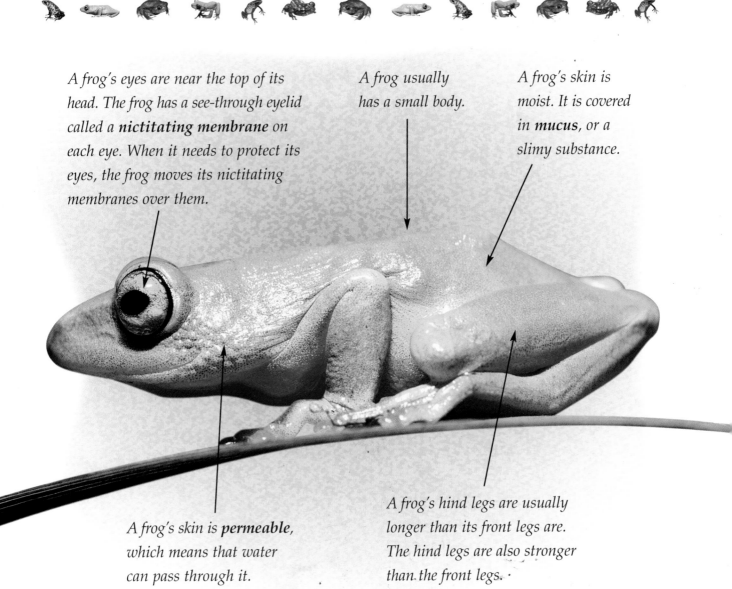

*A frog's eyes are near the top of its head. The frog has a see-through eyelid called a **nictitating membrane** on each eye. When it needs to protect its eyes, the frog moves its nictitating membranes over them.*

A frog usually has a small body.

*A frog's skin is moist. It is covered in **mucus**, or a slimy substance.*

*A frog's skin is **permeable**, which means that water can pass through it.*

A frog's hind legs are usually longer than its front legs are. The hind legs are also stronger than the front legs.

Frog skin

Frogs must breathe **oxygen** to stay alive. Oxygen is a gas that is in air and in water. Most adult frogs breathe air using lungs. Some frogs can also **absorb**, or take in, oxygen through **pores**, or tiny holes, in their skin. In order to absorb oxygen, a frog's skin must be wet. As well as oxygen, frogs absorb water through their skin. Like all animals, frogs need water to stay alive.

15

Frog food

Frogs are **predators**. Predators are animals that hunt and eat other animals. The animals that predators eat are called **prey**. Frogs are important animals in many **food chains**. A food chain is a pattern of eating and being eaten. For example, many insects eat plants, and frogs eat insects. Frogs hunt and eat many other kinds of prey, such as snails, small fish, spiders, and worms. In turn, frogs are eaten by many birds, **mammals**, and other animals. Hawks, owls, lizards, snakes, and foxes all eat frogs. Some of these animals feed on tadpoles and frog eggs, too.

This bullfrog is eating a worm.

Sticky business

Most frogs have long, sticky tongues. To catch prey, a frog usually sits very still and waits for an animal to come near enough to catch. The frog flicks out its tongue quickly. The prey sticks to the frog's tongue, and the frog quickly pulls its tongue back into its mouth. The frog then swallows the prey whole.

It takes less than one second for a frog to flick out its sticky tongue and pull it back in again! This frog is using its tongue to catch a damselfly.

Losing their habitats

One of the greatest dangers to frogs is **habitat loss**. Habitat loss is the destruction of the natural areas in which animals live and find food. Each year, the number of people on Earth increases. People need more space for homes, farms, and roads. People **drain**, or remove the water from, wetlands. They then fill the wetlands with dirt to create more farmland on which to plant **crops**. Crops are plants that people grow for food. People also **clear**, or remove the trees and other plants from, rain forests and other forests. When people clear forests, they destroy the homes of animals. Many frogs lose their habitats and their sources of food.

Trampled ground

Every year, people use large areas of land to raise **livestock**, or farm animals such as cows. The livestock walk over the land as they **graze**, or eat grass and other plants. They sometimes graze near ponds, streams, and other bodies of water. As they graze, the animals trample the muddy ground and destroy some of the plants. Trampling on the soft ground also wears away the **banks** of the ponds and streams, where frogs live. Banks are the lands alongside bodies of water. The livestock destroy frog habitats and leave even fewer places for frogs to live, find food, and lay eggs.

The Ramsey Canyon leopard frog is critically endangered. One of the reasons it is critically endangered is that its habitat is being destroyed by grazing livestock.

Chemical concerns

Some people use chemicals, including **pesticides** and **fertilizers**, on their crops, gardens, and fields. These chemicals get into the water and soil and damage frog habitats. As frogs absorb oxygen and moisture through their skin, they also absorb the harmful chemicals, which can cause them to become sick or to die.

When tadpoles and the embryos inside frog eggs absorb the chemicals, they may also die. The embryos and tadpoles that do survive often do not grow properly. Frogs that do not develop properly may not be able to mate and lay eggs. When frogs cannot mate and lay eggs, frog **populations** do not increase.

If there are too many chemicals in this bullfrog tadpole's habitat, its body may not grow properly. As a frog, it will likely not have healthy babies of its own.

Wrong rain

Acid rain is a major threat to frogs. Acid rain is rain that mixes with **pollution** in the air. Pollution is harmful materials, such as chemicals or waste, that make the air, water, and land unclean. When acid rain pours down and flows into lakes, rivers, streams, ponds, and other frog habitats, it can harm frogs, tadpoles, and frog eggs.

Sick and tired

Pesticides, fertilizers, and acid rain can also make the bodies of frogs weak and unhealthy. Frogs are more likely to catch diseases if they have weak, unhealthy bodies. Unhealthy frogs may not be able to mate and lay eggs.

This frog could become sick from pollution in its habitat.

Rays of danger

Frogs with weak bodies are more likely to be harmed by **UVB radiation**. UVB radiation is harmful rays from the sun that are dangerous to all living things, including frogs.

A "hole" lot of trouble

All living things are exposed to UVB radiation because there is a hole in the Earth's **ozone layer**. The hole is slowly getting larger. Scientists have discovered that the amount of UVB radiation that is reaching Earth's surface has increased during the last 30 years. Increased amounts of UVB radiation can weaken the **immune systems** of frogs. It can also kill frogs directly.

Being exposed to UVB radiation makes it harder for this poison arrow frog to fight off diseases and illnesses.

Full threat

Many researchers believe that UVB radiation is a threat to frogs at all stages of their life cycles. Frog eggs do not have hard shells, as many other animal eggs have. As a result, the embryos developing inside the eggs have no protection against UVB radiation. The radiation passes through the jelly-covered eggs and causes some embryos to die. Tadpoles and frogs have thin, delicate skin that absorbs UVB radiation. The UVB radiation can make frogs sick or may even kill them.

Each year, many frogs, tadpoles, and embryos get sick or die because they have no protection from UVB radiation. These Ramsey Canyon leopard frog eggs are being exposed to UVB radiation.

Global warming

When people use **fossil fuels** such as oil and gasoline in their homes and cars, the amount of **carbon dioxide** in the air increases. High levels of carbon dioxide help cause **global warming**. Global warming is the gradual increase of the Earth's temperature. Global warming is a threat to frogs and all living things. As Earth's temperature increases, many swamps and ponds become shallow or dry. Frog eggs and tadpoles cannot survive without enough water. As a result, the populations of frogs cannot grow. If temperatures continue to rise, many species of frogs may disappear from Earth.

The Oregon spotted frog is vulnerable. It lays its eggs in water that is between two and four inches (5-10 cm) deep. If the water level changes, the embryos may not survive.

A fungus among us

Some scientists believe that warmer temperatures also cause **fungi** to grow in frog habitats. Fungi are plantlike living things that feed on living and dead things. Chytrid fungus is a serious threat to certain frogs. The fungus lives in the skin of frogs and may make it difficult for frogs to breathe. The fungus may even be poisonous to frogs.

Spreading a fungus

Many frogs and tadpoles die after they are infected with chytrid fungus. Others can have the fungus and be healthy. Healthy frogs can easily spread the fungus to other frogs, however. Frogs all over the world have died from chytrid fungus.

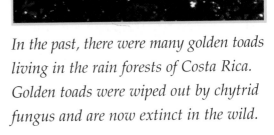

In the past, there were many golden toads living in the rain forests of Costa Rica. Golden toads were wiped out by chytrid fungus and are now extinct in the wild.

25

Other dangers

People threaten frogs by adding **introduced species** into frog habitats. An introduced species is a type of animal that does not normally live in a habitat but has been placed there by people. To fish for sport, people place rainbow trout, golden trout, and brown trout into lakes and ponds in North America. The trout eat large numbers of the tadpoles and frogs that normally live in these habitats. In certain places, the populations of frogs have declined as a result of the introduced species in their habitats.

The population of the mountain yellow-legged frog has declined because of introduced species in its habitat.

Frog foes

People all over the world capture frogs from the wild and sell them as pets. In many countries, it is **illegal**, or against the law, for people to sell and keep certain frogs as pets. People continue to break these laws, however. If people continue to capture and sell rare species, the populations of these frogs will decline even more.

Frog for food

Frog legs are a popular food in certain countries in Europe, North America, and Asia. Some of the frogs that are sold for food are raised on farms and then killed and sold to markets and stores. Other frogs are captured from the wild. When people buy frog legs to eat, they cause more frogs to be killed.

Some people sell frog legs at markets. People only eat the hind legs of frogs. The rest of the bodies are thrown away.

Friends to frogs

The governments of many countries have created laws to protect frogs and their habitats. People are realizing how much we can learn from frogs. For example, frogs are extremely sensitive to even the slightest changes in their habitats.

They often react to these changes sooner than other animals in the habitats do. If frogs are getting sick or dying in certain habitats, it may be a sign that those habitats are polluted. Polluted habitats are not safe for other animals or for people.

*The body of this northern leopard frog is **deformed**, or not formed properly. A researcher is studying the frog to learn how to prevent other frogs from becoming deformed.*

Set to survive

Conservation groups, such as the Amphibian Research Center, are dedicated to protecting frogs. These groups **breed** endangered frogs in **captivity**. To breed means to cause animals to mate and have babies. Breeding frogs in captivity helps ensure that these animals survive. It also gives researchers the opportunity to learn more about frogs.

*The Panamanian golden frog lives in **national parks** in Panama. A national park is an area of land and water that is protected by a government.*

Keeping tabs

There are other organizations, such as Frogwatch USA and the Global Amphibian Assessment, which collect information about frogs and other amphibians and keep close track of the populations of these animals. The information can also be used to educate people about the dangers to frogs and about how people can protect them.

You can help!

Frogs need your help! You can help save frogs by keeping the environment clean. Ask your parents to stop using pesticides and fertilizers in their gardens and yards. Ask your family and neighbors to use less kitchen, laundry, and bathroom cleaners and fewer chemicals in their swimming pools.

Take a walk!

You and your parents can help stop global warming by walking or riding bicycles instead of using a car to travel from place to place. Turning off your computers, stereos, and television sets when you are not using them is also helpful.

If you want to see frogs up close, take a trip to a zoo. You may see a blue poison frog just like this one!

Fun frog facts

You can also help frogs by getting other people interested in them. You can begin by learning some fascinating frog facts and sharing what you learn with your friends and family. For example, one of the world's smallest frogs is less than a half inch (1.3 cm) long. The largest frog on Earth is the Goliath frog, which can grow to be two feet (0.6 m) long! The more you learn and share information about frogs, the more fascinated you will become. Ask your friends and family to tell others about frogs, too.

Frogs online

There is plenty of information about frogs online. These websites will get you started:

- www.nwf.org/frogwatchUSA
- cgee.hamline.edu/frogs
- frogs.org.au

Glossary

Note: Boldfaced words that are defined in the text may not appear in the glossary.

captivity A state of living in an enclosed area such as a zoo

carbon dioxode A gas made up of carbon and oxygen that is present in air

conservation groups People who join together to protect and save living things

continent One of the seven large areas of land on Earth—Africa, Antarctica, Asia, Australia, Europe, North America, and South America

fertilizers Chemicals that people add to soil to help plants grow

gills Body parts found in fish and tadpoles that take in oxygen from water

grassland An area that is covered mainly with grass and shrubs

immune system The body system that protects animals from diseases

lungs The organs some animals use to breathe oxygen from air

mammals Warm-blooded animals that give birth to live babies

ozone layer A layer of gas in the Earth's atmosphere that blocks UVB radiation

pesticides Chemicals that people use to kill insects

population The total number of one species of plant or animal living in a certain area

webbed Describing an animal's foot that has skin between each of the toes

Index

1 2 3 4 5 6 7 8 9 0   Printed in the U.S.A.   5 4 3 2 1 0 9 8 7 6